Table of Contents

Welcome	Page 1
What Are the Benefits and Responsibilities of Citizenship?	Page 3
Frequently Asked Questions	Page 5
Who Is Eligible for Naturalization?	Page 17
Table of Eligibility Requirements	Page 18
Time as a Permanent Resident	Page 22
Continuous Residence	Page 22
Physical Presence in the United States	Page 23
Time as a Resident in a USCIS District or State	Page 24
Good Moral Character	Page 25
English and Civics	Page 26
Attachment to the Constitution	Page 28
What Should I Expect From the Naturalization Process?	Page 31
Preparing to Apply	Page 32
Completing Your Application and Getting Photographed	Page 33
Getting Fingerprinted	Page 35
Being Interviewed	Page 36
Taking the Oath	Page 38
What Kind of Customer Service Can I Expect?	Page 41
Where Do I Go for Help?	Page 43
Glossary of Terms	Page 45

A Guide to Naturalization

This page is intentionally left blank.

Welcome

E Pluribus Unum - Out of Many, One

-Motto inscripted on the Great Seal of the United States

Welcome

We are very pleased that you want to become a U.S. citizen. The United States is a nation of immigrants. Throughout our history, immigrants have come here seeking a better way of life and have strengthened our Nation in the process.

For more than 200 years, the United States has remained strong because of our citizens and the common civic values we share. Deciding to become a U.S. citizen is one of the most important decisions in a person's life. If you decide to apply for naturalization, you will be showing your permanent commitment to the United States. You will also be showing your loyalty to its Constitution and its people.

When you are naturalized, you agree to accept all of the responsibilities of being a citizen. You agree to support the United States, its Constitution, and its laws. In return, you are rewarded with all the rights and privileges that are part of citizenship. We welcome your interest and hope you will read on to learn more about naturalization.

What Is Naturalization?

Naturalization is commonly referred to as the manner in which a person not born in the United States voluntarily becomes a U.S. citizen.

What Is This *Guide* for?

U.S. Citizenship and Immigration Services (USCIS) created this *Guide* to provide better and more consistent information to people interested in naturalization. It is written mainly for people 18 years or older who want to become citizens. Please take the time to review this information to make sure that you are eligible to apply for naturalization. You can find more information at **www.uscis.gov** or by calling Customer Service at **1-800-375-5283** or **1-800-767-1833** (for hearing impaired).

This page is intentionally left blank.

What Are the Benefits and Responsibilities of Citizenship?

Benefits

The Constitution and laws of the United States give many rights to both citizens and non-citizens living in the United States. However, some rights are only for citizens, such as:

- **Voting.** Only U.S. citizens can vote in Federal elections. Most States also restrict the right to vote, in most elections, to U.S. citizens.

- **Bringing family members to the United States.** Citizens generally get priority when petitioning to bring family members permanently to this country.

- **Obtaining citizenship for children born abroad.** In most cases, a child born abroad to a U.S. citizen is automatically a U.S. citizen.

- **Traveling with a U.S. passport.** A U.S. passport allows you to get assistance from the U.S. government when overseas.

- **Becoming eligible for Federal jobs.** Most jobs with government agencies require U.S. citizenship.

- **Becoming an elected official.** Many elected offices in this country require U.S. citizenship.

- **Showing your patriotism.** In addition, becoming a U.S. citizen is a way to demonstrate your commitment to your new country.

The above list does not include all the benefits of citizenship, only some of the more important ones.

Responsibilities

To become a U.S. citizen you must take the Oath of Allegiance. The oath includes several promises you make when you become a U.S. citizen, including promises to:

- Give up all prior allegiance to any other nation or sovereignty;

- Swear allegiance to the United States;

- Support and defend the Constitution and the laws of the United States; and

- Serve the country when required.

U.S. citizens have many responsibilities other than the ones mentioned in the Oath. Citizens have a responsibility to participate in the political process by registering and voting in elections. Serving on a jury is another responsibility of citizenship. Finally, America becomes stronger when all of its citizens respect the different opinions, cultures, ethnic groups, and religions found in this country. Tolerance for differences is also a responsibility of citizenship.

When you decide to become a U.S. citizen, you should be willing to fulfill the responsibilities of citizenship. We hope you will honor and respect the freedoms and opportunities citizenship gives you. At the same time, we hope you become an active member of your community. It is by participating in your community that you truly become an American.

A Guide to Naturalization

This page is intentionally left blank.

Frequently Asked Questions

Q 1. How can I become a U.S. citizen?

A You may become a U.S. citizen **(1)** by birth or **(2)** through naturalization.

Q 2. Who is born a U.S. citizen?

A Generally, people are born U.S. citizens if they are born in the United States or if they are born to U.S. citizens:

(1) If you were born in the United States:
Normally you were a U.S. citizen at birth.[1] (Including, in most cases, the Commonwealth of Puerto Rico, the territories of Guam and the U.S. Virgin Islands, and after November 4, 1986, the Commonwealth of the Northern Mariana Islands),

(2) If you were born abroad to TWO U.S. citizens:
And at least one of your parents lived in the United States at some point in his or her life, **then in most cases you are a U.S. citizen**.

(3) If you were born abroad to ONE U.S. citizen:
In most cases, you are a U.S. citizen if **all** of the following are true:

- One of your parents was a U.S. citizen when you were born;

- Your citizen parent lived at least 5 years in the United States before you were born; and

- At least 2 of those 5 years in the United States were after your citizen parent's 14th birthday.[2]

Your record of birth abroad, if registered with a U.S. consulate or embassy, is proof of your citizenship. You may also apply for a passport to have your citizenship recognized. If you need additional proof of your citizenship, you may file an "Application for Certificate of Citizenship" (Form N-600) with USCIS to get a Certificate of Citizenship. Call the USCIS Forms Line at **1-800-870-3676** to request Form N-600, or download the form at **www.uscis.gov**.

---

[1] The exception is persons who were born not subject to the jurisdiction of the United States, such as children of foreign diplomats.

[2] If you were born before November 14, 1986, you are a citizen if your U.S. citizen parent lived in the United States for at least 10 years and 5 of those years in the United States were after your citizen parent's 14th birthday.

3. How do I become a naturalized citizen?

 If you are not a U.S. citizen by birth or did not acquire/derive U.S. citizenship automatically after birth, you may still be eligible to become a citizen through the naturalization process. Eligible persons use the "Application for Naturalization" (Form N-400) to apply for naturalization.

Persons who acquired citizenship from parent(s) while under 18 years of age use the "Application for Certificate of Citizenship" (Form N-600) to document their citizenship. Qualified children who reside abroad use the "Application for Citizenship and Issuance of Certificate under Section 322" (Form N-600K) to document their naturalization. You may call the USCIS Forms Line at **1-800-870-3676** to request a Form N-400, N-600, or N-600K; or you may download all of these forms at **www.uscis.gov**.

 4. What are the requirements for naturalization?

 Please see Section 4, "Who Is Eligible For Naturalization?," beginning on page 17 for more details on the eligibility requirements for naturalization. You should also complete the Eligibility Worksheet in the back of this *Guide* to help you find out if you meet the eligibility requirements.

5. When does my time as a Permanent Resident begin?

 Your time as a Permanent Resident begins on the date you were granted permanent resident status. This date is on your Permanent Resident Card (formerly known as an Alien Registration Card or "Green Card"). The sample cards on this page show where you can find important information such as the date your Permanent Residence began.

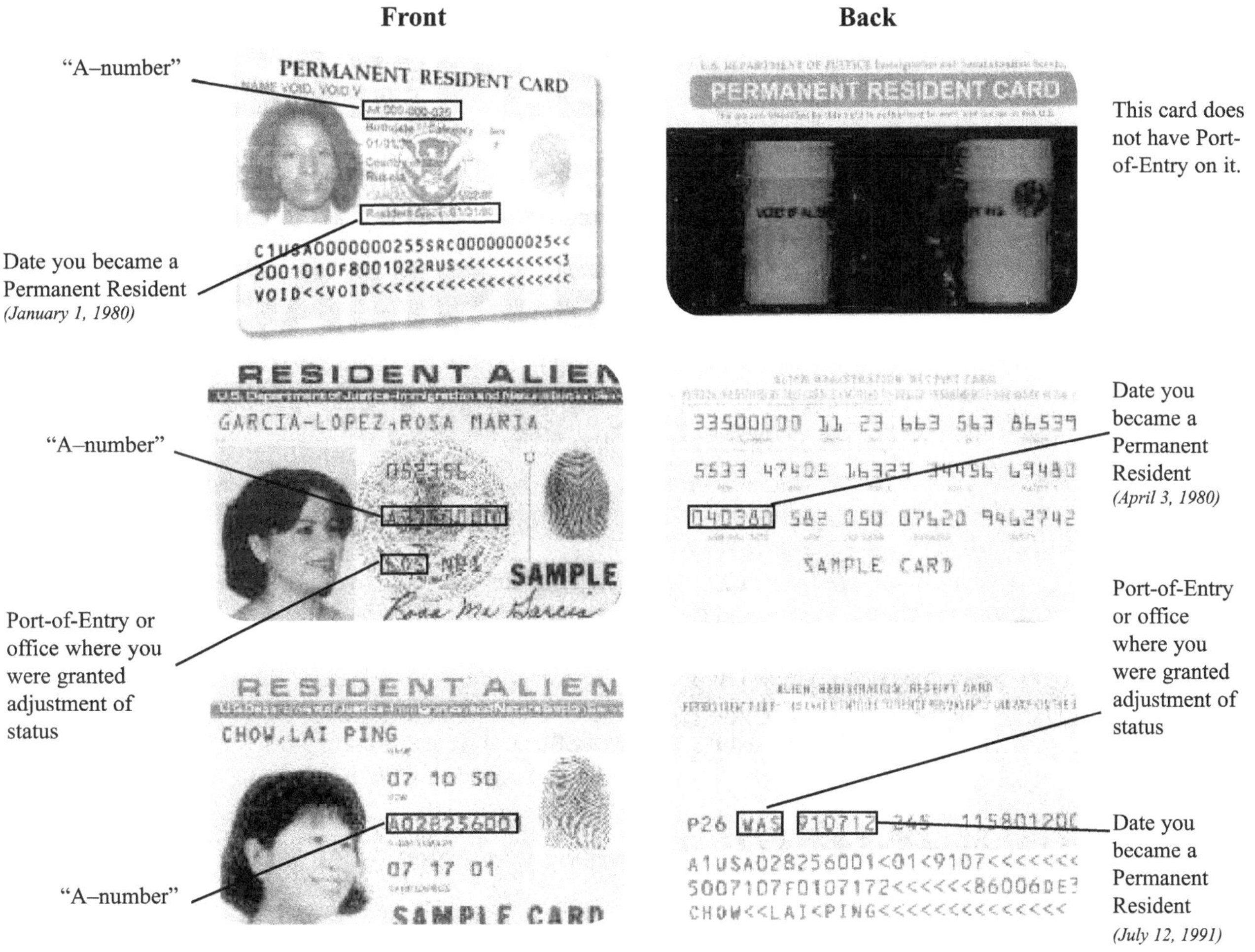

Front | Back

"A–number"

Date you became a Permanent Resident
(January 1, 1980)

This card does not have Port-of-Entry on it.

"A–number"

Port-of-Entry or office where you were granted adjustment of status

Date you became a Permanent Resident
(April 3, 1980)

Port-of-Entry or office where you were granted adjustment of status

"A–number"

Date you became a Permanent Resident
(July 12, 1991)

NOTE: The "A–number" is the Alien Registration Number

A Guide to Naturalization

6. What form do I use to file for naturalization?

 You should use an "Application for Naturalization" (Form N-400). Call the USCIS Forms Line at **1-800-870-3676** to request Form N-400. You may also download the form at **www.uscis.gov**.

 7. If I have been convicted of a crime but my record has been expunged, do I need to write that on my application or tell a USCIS officer?

 Yes. You should always be honest with USCIS about all:

- Arrests (even if you were not charged or convicted);
- Convictions (even if your record was cleared or expunged);
- Crimes you have committed for which you were not arrested or convicted; and
- Any countervailing evidence, or evidence in your favor concerning the circumstances of your arrests, and/or convictions or offenses that you would like USCIS to consider.

Even if you have committed a minor crime, USCIS may deny your application if you do not tell the USCIS officer about the incident. Note that unless a traffic incident was alcohol or drug related, you do not need to submit documentation for traffic fines and incidents that did not involve an actual arrest if the only penalty was a fine less than **$500** and/or points on your driver's license.

 8. Where do I file my naturalization application?

 You should send your completed "Application for Naturalization" (Form N-400) to the appropriate USCIS Lockbox Facility that serves your area, see page 34 for detailed instructions. Also see page 34 for separate filing instructions for members of the Armed Forces and the spouses of active members of the Armed Forces. Remember to make a copy of your application. **Do not** send original documents with your application unless the Document Checklist included with this *Guide* states that an original is required. **Always** make copies of documents that you send to USCIS.

 9. Will USCIS help me, or make accommodations for me, if I have a disability?

 USCIS will make every effort to make reasonable accommodations for applicants with disabilities who need modifications to the naturalization process in order to demonstrate their eligibility. For example, if you use a wheelchair, we will make sure you can be fingerprinted, interviewed, and sworn in at a location that is wheelchair accessible. If you are hearing impaired, the officer conducting your interview will speak loudly and slowly, or we will work with you to arrange for an American sign language interpreter. If you require an American sign language interpreter at the oath ceremony, please indicate that in your Form N-400 in the section where you are asked if you need an accommodation for a disability. If you use a service animal such as a guide dog, your animal may come with you to your interview and oath ceremony.

We are continuing to work on better ways to make the naturalization process easier for applicants with disabilities. If you know in advance that you will need some kind of accommodation, write a letter explaining what you will need and send it to the USCIS district office that will interview you after you receive your interview notice. If you have a physical or developmental disability or a mental impairment so severe that you cannot acquire or demonstrate the required knowledge of English and civics, you may be eligible for an exemption of those requirements. To request an exemption, you must file a "Medical Certification for Disability Exceptions" (Form N-648). See page 26 of this *Guide* for more information.

10. Where is my local USCIS office?

To find the local USCIS office that serves your area, please use the field office locator at **www.uscis.gov**.

11. What is the fee for processing an application?*

The current fee for processing a naturalization application can be found on the single page titled "Current Naturalization Fees" in the back of this *Guide*. If you are under 75 years old, you must also pay a fee to have your fingerprints taken.**

12. How can I pay my application fee?

You must send the fee with your application. Pay the fee with a check or money order drawn on a U.S. bank payable to the **Department of Homeland Security**. Do not use the initials DHS or USDHS. **Do Not Send Cash**.

Residents of Guam should make the fee payable to the "Treasurer, Guam," and residents of the U.S. Virgin Islands should make the fee payable to the "Commissioner of Finance of the Virgin Islands."

Fees for biometric services, which include your photograph and signature, are separate from your application fee. Remember that your application fee is not refundable even if you withdraw your application or if your case is denied.

* If you are applying for naturalization based on your own service in the Armed Forces of the United States, no filing fee is required. Please see "Naturalization Information for Military Personnel" (Form M-599) for more information.
** If you are 75 years or older, or if you are filing on the basis of your service in the Armed Forces of the United States, or if you are filing from abroad, **do not** send the biometric services fee for fingerprinting with your application.

Q 13. How long will it take to become naturalized?

A The time it takes to be naturalized varies by location. USCIS is continuing to modernize and improve the naturalization process and would like to decrease the time it takes to an average of 6 months after the Form N-400 is filed.

Q 14. Where can I be fingerprinted?

A After we receive your application, we will tell you where you should get fingerprinted. For more information about fingerprinting, see page 35.

Q 15. How do I find out the status of my naturalization application?

A You may check the status of your naturalization application by visiting **www.uscis.gov** or by calling Customer Service at **1-800-375-5283 (TTY: 1-800-767-1833)**.

Q 16. What if I cannot go to my scheduled interview?

A It is very important not to miss your interview. If you have to miss your interview, you should write the office where your interview is to be conducted as soon as possible and ask to have your interview rescheduled. Rescheduling an interview may add several months to the naturalization process, so make all attempts to attend your original interview date.

If you miss your scheduled interview without notifying USCIS, we will "administratively close" your case. If we close your case because you missed your interview, we will notify you at your last address of record. Unless you contact us to schedule a new interview within 1 year after we close your case, we will deny your application.

17. What do I do if my address has changed?

 It is important that USCIS has your most current address. If we do not, you may not receive important information from us. For example, we may not be able to notify you about the date and time of your interview or about additional documents you may need to send or bring.

If you move after filing your "Application for Naturalization" (Form N-400), call Customer Service at **1-800-375-5283 (TTY: 1-800-767-1833)** to change your address on your pending Form N-400. Every time you move, you are required by law to inform USCIS of your new address. To meet this legal requirement, you must file an "Alien's Change of Address Card" (Form AR-11), in addition to calling Customer Service. You must file the Form AR-11 within 10 days of your move. There is no fee to file this form. You should also notify the U.S. Postal Service of your new address to help ensure that any mail already on its way may be forwarded to you.

 18. Can I change my name when I naturalize?

 Congress did not give USCIS legal authority to change a person's name when that person naturalizes. Therefore, there are only two ways that USCIS can issue your Certificate of Naturalization under a new name:

1. If you present proof that you have already changed your name according to the legal requirements that apply to persons living in your State, USCIS can issue the Certificate of Naturalization with your new name. Such proof might include a marriage certificate or divorce decree showing that you changed your name when you married or divorced. It might also include some other State court order establishing that you changed your name.

2. If you are going to take the Oath of Allegiance at a Naturalization Ceremony that is held in Court, you may ask the Court to change your name. If the Court grants your request, your new name will appear on your Certificate of Naturalization.

 19. If USCIS grants me naturalization, when will I become a citizen?

 You become a citizen as soon as you take the Oath of Allegiance to the United States in a formal naturalization ceremony. In some places, you can choose to take the oath the same day as your interview. If that option is not available, or if you prefer a ceremony at a later date, USCIS will notify you of the ceremony date with a "Notice of Naturalization Oath Ceremony" (Form N-445).

20. What should I do if I cannot go to my oath ceremony?

 If you cannot go to the oath ceremony, you should return the "Notice of Naturalization Oath Ceremony" (Form N-445) that you received to your local USCIS office. Include a letter saying why you cannot go to the ceremony. Make a copy of the notice and your letter before you send them to USCIS. Your local USCIS office will reschedule you and send you a new "Notice of Naturalization Oath Ceremony" (Form N-445) to tell you when your ceremony will be.

 21. What can I do if USCIS denies my application?

 If you think that USCIS was wrong to deny your naturalization application, you may request a hearing with an immigration officer. Your denial letter will explain how to request a hearing and will include the form you need. The form for filing an appeal is the "Request for Hearing on a Decision in Naturalization Proceedings under Section 336 of the INA" (Form N-336). You must file the form, including the correct fee, to USCIS within 30 days after you receive a denial letter.

If, after an appeal hearing with USCIS, you still believe you have been wrongly denied naturalization, you may file a petition for a new review of your application in U.S. District Court.

 22. Can I reapply for naturalization if USCIS denies my application?

 In many cases, you may reapply. If you reapply, you will need to complete and resubmit a new Form N-400 and pay the fee again. You will also need to have your fingerprints and photographs taken again. If your application is denied, the denial letter should indicate the date you may reapply for citizenship.

If you are denied because you failed the English or civics test, you may reapply for naturalization as soon as you want. You should reapply whenever you believe you have learned enough English or civics to pass both tests.

23. What do I do if I lose my Certificate of Naturalization? What do I use as proof of citizenship if I do not have my certificate?

You may get a new Certificate of Naturalization by submitting an "Application for Replacement Naturalization/Citizenship Document" (Form N-565) to USCIS. You may request Form N-565 by calling the USCIS Forms Line **(1-800-870-3676)**, or by downloading the form at **www.uscis.gov**. Submit this form with the appropriate fee to the Nebraska or Texas Service Center, depending on which Service Center has jurisdiction over your residence.

If you have one, you may use your U.S. passport as evidence of citizenship while you wait for a replacement certificate. It is strongly recommended that you apply for a passport as soon as you become a citizen.

 24. If my Permanent Resident Card expires while I am applying for naturalization, do I still need to apply for a new card?

If you apply for naturalization **6 months or more before** the expiration date on your Permanent Resident Card (formerly known as an Alien Registration Card or "Green Card"), you do not have to apply for a new card. However, you may apply for a renewal card if you wish by using an "Application to Replace Permanent Resident Card" (Form I-90) and paying the appropriate fee. Call the USCIS Forms Line or visit **www.uscis.gov**.

If you apply for naturalization **less than 6 months before** the expiration date on your Permanent Resident Card, or do not apply for naturalization until your card has already expired, you must renew your card.

 25. If I am a U.S. citizen, is my child a U.S. citizen?

 A child who is born in the United States, or born abroad to a U.S. citizen(s) who lived in (or came to) the United States for the required period of time prior to the child's birth, is generally considered a U.S. citizen at birth.

A child who is:

- Born to a U.S. citizen who did not live in (or come to) the United States for the required period of time prior to the child's birth, or

- Born to one U.S. citizen parent and one alien parent or two alien parents who naturalize after the child's birth, or

- Adopted (stepchildren cannot derive or acquire citizenship through their stepparents) and is permanently residing in the United States can become a U.S. citizen by action of law on the date on which all of the following requirements have been met:

- The child was lawfully admitted for permanent residence*; and

- Either parent was a United States citizen by birth or naturalization**; and

- The child was still under 18 years of age; and

- The child was not married; and

- The child was the parent's legitimate child or was legitimated by the parent before the child's 16th birthday (children born out of wedlock who were not legitimated before their 16th birthday do **not** derive United States citizenship through their father); and

- If adopted, the child met the requirements of section 101(b)(1)(E) or (F) of the Immigration and Nationality Act (INA) and has had a full and final adoption; and

- The child was residing in the United States in the legal custody of the U.S. citizen parent (this includes joint custody); and

- The child was residing in the United States in the physical custody of the U.S. citizen parent.

If you and your child meet all of these requirements, you may obtain a U.S. passport for the child as evidence of citizenship. If the child needs further evidence of citizenship, you may submit an "Application for Certificate of Citizenship" (Form N-600) to USCIS to obtain a Certificate of Citizenship. **(NOTE:** A child who meets these requirements before his or her 18th birthday may obtain a passport or Certificate of Citizenship at any time, even after he or she turns 18.)

*NOTE – Children who immigrated under the "IR-3" or "IR-4" categories must have had an immigrant petition filed on their behalf before their 16th birthday; see answers to Question 26. All adoptions for any other type of immigration benefit, including naturalization, must be completed by the child's 16th birthday, with one exception: A child adopted while under the age of 18 years by the same parents who adopted a natural sibling who met the usual requirements.

**NOTE – The "one U.S. citizen parent" rule applies only to children who first fulfilled the requirements for automatic citizenship (other than at birth abroad) on or after February 27, 2001. In order to qualify for automatic citizenship (other than at birth abroad) on or before February 26, 2001, both of the child's parents must have been United States citizens either at birth or through naturalization—both parents if the child had two parents; the surviving parent if a parent had died; the parent with legal custody if the parents were divorced or legally separated; or the mother only, if the child had been born out of wedlock and the child's paternity had not been established by legitimation.

26. If I am a U.S. citizen, but my child does not meet the requirements listed above, can I still apply for citizenship for my child?

A child who is regularly residing **in** the United States can become a citizen of the United States **only** by meeting the requirements listed in the answer to Question 25. If a child regularly resides **in** the United States and is not a lawful permanent resident, he or she cannot acquire citizenship automatically until he or she is granted lawful permanent residence. If a child who has been lawfully admitted for permanent residence fails to qualify for citizenship under the provisions of law, he or she may apply for naturalization after reaching 18 years of age by filing Form N-400, provided that he or she has the required 5 years of lawful permanent residence.

U.S. citizens with children by birth or adoption (stepchildren do not qualify) who do **not** regularly reside in the United States, may apply for citizenship for such a child if all of the following conditions are met:

- The child is under 18 years of age; and

- The child is not married; and

- The child regularly resides outside the United States; and

- The child is temporarily present in the United States pursuant to a lawful admission and is maintaining such lawful status; and

- The child is in legal and physical custody of a parent who is a U.S. citizen; and

- The child is the U.S. citizen's legitimate child, or was legitimated before the child's 16th birthday (children born out of wedlock who were not legitimated before their 16th birthday may be eligible for this procedure through his or her mother); and

- If adopted, the child meets the requirements of section 101(b)(1)(E) or (F) of the INA and had a full and final adoption; and

- Either of the following is true:

    - The citizen parent has lived at least 5 years in the United States, and at least 2 of which were after the citizen parent's 14th birthday; or

    - If the child's citizen parent has not lived in the United States for at least 5 years, 2 of which were after that parent's 14th birthday, the citizen parent currently has a parent (the child's grandparent) who:

        - Is also a U.S. citizen; and

        - Lived in the United States for 5 years, at least 2 of which were after the citizen grandparent's 14th birthday; and

        - Is living or deceased at the time of the adjudication of the application and the taking of the oath.

If the foregoing conditions are met, the citizen parent can apply for citizenship and a Certificate of Citizenship on behalf of the child using an "Application for Citizenship and Issuance of a Certificate under Section 322" (Form N-600K). Both the citizen parent and the child must appear at an interview with a USCIS officer in the United States. The child must meet **all** of the required conditions at the time he or she takes the Oath of Allegiance. (**NOTE:** The oath may be waived if the child is too young to understand it.)

A Guide to Naturalization

This page is intentionally left blank.

Who Is Eligible for Naturalization?

Naturalization is how immigrants become citizens of the United States. If you wish to apply for naturalization, you should use the "Application for Naturalization" (Form N-400).

If you want to apply for citizenship for a child who is under 18 years old, you should use the "Application for Certificate of Citizenship" (Form N-600) or "Application for Citizenship and Issuance of a Certificate under Section 322" (Form N-600K). For more information about applying for citizenship for your children, see Questions 25-26 on pages 13-15.

In the next few pages, we describe the naturalization eligibility requirements for persons who will use Form N-400.

The following table summarizes the naturalization requirements for *most* types of applicants. After the table is a section that provides more information on each requirement. If you still have questions about your eligibility, you should consult an immigrant assistance organization or USCIS.

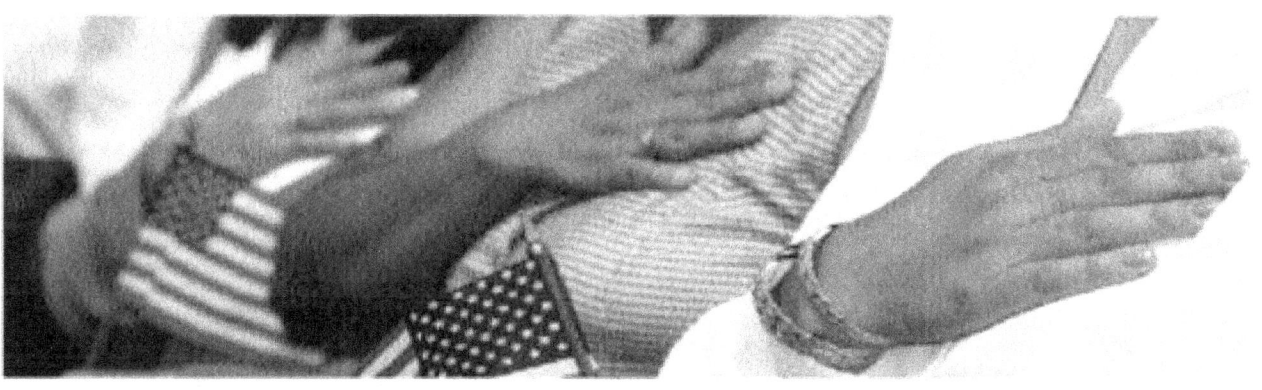

REQUIREMENTS

TYPE OF APPLICANT	 **Time as Permanent Resident**	**Continuous Residence**
If you are at least 18 years old and: Have been a Permanent Resident for the past 5 years and have no special circumstances. *NOTE: Over 90% of applicants fall into this category.*	5 years	5 years as a Permanent Resident without leaving the United States for trips of 6 months or longer.
If you are at least 18 years old and: Are currently married to and living with a U.S. citizen; **and** Have been married to and living with that same U.S. citizen for the past 3 years; **and** Your spouse has been a U.S. citizen for the past 3 years.	3 years	3 years as a Permanent Resident without leaving the United States for trips of 6 months or longer.
If you: Are in the U.S. Armed Forces (or will be filing your application within 6 months of an honorable discharge); **and** Have served for at least 1 year.	You must be a Permanent Resident on the day of your interview.	Not Required
If you are at least 18 years old and: Were in the U.S. Armed Forces for less than 1 year **or** **If you are at least 18 years old and:** Were in the U.S. Armed Forces for 1 year or more, but you were discharged more than 6 months ago	5 years	5 years as a Permanent Resident without leaving the United States for trips of 6 months or longer. *NOTE: If you were out of the country as part of your service, this time out of the country does not break your continuous residence. It is treated just like time spent in the United States. See "Naturalization Information for Military Personnel" (Form M-599) for more information.*
If you: Performed active duty military service during: • World War I (April 6, 1917-November 11, 1918); • World War II (September 1, 1939-December 31, 1946); • Korea (June 25, 1950-July 1, 1955); • Vietnam (February 28, 1961-October 15, 1978); • Persian Gulf (August 2, 1990-April 11, 1991); or • On or after September 11, 2001.	You are not required to be a Permanent Resident. *NOTE: If you did not enlist or reenlist in the United States or its outlying possessions, you must be a Permanent Resident on the day you file your application.*	Not Required
If you are at least 18 years old and: Were married to a U.S. citizen who died during a period of honorable active duty service in the U.S. Armed Forces. *NOTE: You must have been married to and living with your U.S. citizen spouse at the time of his/her death.*	You must be a Permanent Resident on the day of your interview.	Not Required
If you are at least 18 years old and: • Are a U.S. national (a non-citizen who owes permanent allegiance to the United States); **and** • Have become a resident of any State; **and** • Are otherwise qualified for naturalization.	You are not required to be a Permanent Resident.	The same requirements as any other applicant for naturalization, depending on your qualifications. *NOTE: Any time you resided in American Samoa or Swains Island counts the same as the time you resided within a State of the United States.*
▼ **Where to go for more information.**	Page 22	Pages 22-23

	 Physical Presence in the United States	 Time in USCIS District or State	Good Moral Character	 English & Civics Knowledge	 Attachment to the Constitution
	30 months	3 months	Required	Required	Required
	18 months	3 months	Required	Required	Required
	Not Required	Not Required	Required	Required	Required
	30 months **NOTE:** *Time in the U.S. Armed Forces counts as time physically present in the United States no matter where you were. See "Naturalization Information for Military Personnel" (Form M-599) for more information.*	3 months	Required	Required	Required
	Not Required	Not Required	Required	Required	Required
	Not Required	Not Required	Required	Required	Required
	The same requirements as any other applicant for naturalization, depending on your qualifications. **NOTE:** *Any time you resided in American Samoa or Swains Island counts the same as the time you resided within a State of the United States.*	3 months or not required, depending on your qualifications.	Required	Required	Required
	Pages 23-24	Page 24	Page 25	Pages 26-27	Pages 28-29

A Guide to Naturalization

REQUIREMENTS	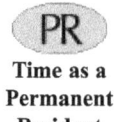 Time as a Permanent Resident	 Continuous Residence
If you are at least 18 years old and: Served on a vessel operated by the United States **or** **If you:** Served on a vessel registered in the United States and owned by U.S. citizens or a U.S. corporation.	5 years	5 years as a Permanent Resident without leaving the United States for trips of 6 months or longer. *NOTE: If you were out of the country while serving on a vessel, this time out of the country does not break your continuous residence. It is treated just like time spent in the United States.*
If you are at least 18 years old and: Are an employee or an individual under contract to the U.S. Government.	5 years	5 years as a Permanent Resident without leaving the United States for trips of 6 months or longer. *NOTE: An absence from the United States for 1 year or more will break your continuous residence. You may keep your continuous residence if you have had at least 1 year of unbroken continuous residence since becoming a Permanent Resident and you get an approved Form N-470 before you have been out of the United States for 1 year.*
If you are at least 18 years old and: Are a person who performs ministerial or priestly functions for a religious denomination or an interdenominational organization with a valid presence in the United States.	5 years	5 years as a Permanent Resident without leaving the United States for trips of 6 months or longer. *NOTE: An absence from the United States for 1 year or more will break your continuous residence. You may keep your continuous residence if you have had at least 1 year of unbroken continuous residence since becoming a Permanent Resident and you get an approved Form N-470 at any time before applying for naturalization.*
If you are at least 18 years old and: Are employed by one of the following: • An American institution of research recognized by the Attorney General; • An American-owned firm or corporation engaged in the development of foreign trade and commerce for the United States; or • A public international organization of which the United States is a member by law or treaty (if the employment began after you became a Permanent Resident).	5 years	5 years as a Permanent Resident without leaving the United States for trips of 6 months or longer. *NOTE: An absence from the United States for 1 year or more will break your continuous residence. You may keep your continuous residence if you have had at least 1 year of unbroken continuous residence since becoming a Permanent Resident and you get an approved Form N-470 before you have been out of the United States for 1 year.*
If you are at least 18 years old and: Have been employed for 5 years or more by a U.S. nonprofit organization that principally promotes the interests of the United States abroad through the communications media.	5 years	Not Required
If you are at least 18 years old and: Are the spouse of a U.S. citizen who is one of the following: • A member of the U.S. Armed Forces; • An employee or an individual under contract to the U.S. Government; • An employee of an American institution of research recognized by the Attorney General; • An employee of an American-owned firm or corporation engaged in the development of foreign trade and commerce for the United States; • An employee of a public international organization of which the United States is a member by law or treaty; or • A person who performs ministerial or priestly functions for a religious denomination or an interdenominational organization with a valid presence in the United States **and** You will be proceeding to join your spouse whose work abroad under orders of the qualifying employer will continue for at least 1 year after the date you will be naturalized. Form N-400 should be filed prior to departing.	You must be a Permanent Resident at the time of your USCIS interview.	Not Required

Where to go for more information.   Page 22   Pages 22-23

Physical Presence in the United States 	Time in USCIS District or State 	Good Moral Character	English & Civics Knowledge 	Attachment to the Constitution 
30 months *NOTE: Time served on the vessel counts as time "physically present" in the United States no matter where you were.*	3 months	Required	Required	Required
30 months *NOTE: Time spent in this type of employment counts as time physically present in the United States no matter where you are as long as you get an approved Form N-470 before you have been out of the United States for 1 year.*	3 months	Required	Required	Required
30 months *NOTE: Time spent in this type of employment counts as time physically present in the United States no matter where you are as long as you get an approved Form N-470 before you apply for naturalization.*	3 months	Required	Required	Required
30 months	3 months	Required	Required	Required
Not Required	Not Required	Required	Required	Required
Not Required	Not Required	Required	Required	Required
Pages 23-24	Page 24	Page 25	Pages 26-27	Pages 28-29

Time as a Permanent Resident

Permanent Residents are people who have "permanent resident" status in the United States as provided for under U.S. immigration laws. Permanent Residents are normally given Permanent Resident Cards, also known as "Green Cards." (**NOTE:** These cards used to be called Alien Registration Cards.)

In most cases, you must be a Permanent Resident for a certain number of years before you may apply for naturalization. But, it is not enough to be a Permanent Resident for the required number of years; you must also be in "continuous residence" during that time.

Continuous Residence

"Continuous residence" means that you have not left the United States for a long period of time. If you leave the United States for too long, you may interrupt your continuous residence.

What if I was outside the United States between 6 and 12 months? If you leave the United States for more than 6 months, but less than 1 year, you have broken or disrupted your continuous residence unless you can prove otherwise. Read the "Document Checklist" in the back of this *Guide* to find out what information you must give to prove you did not break your continuous residence.

What if I was outside the United States for 1 year or longer? In almost all cases, if you leave the United States for 1 year or more, you have disrupted your continuous residence. This is true even if you have a Re-entry Permit.

If you leave the country for 1 year or longer, you may be eligible to re-enter as a Permanent Resident if you have a Re-entry Permit. But none of the time you were in the United States *before you left* the country counts toward your time in continuous residence.

If you return within 2 years, some of your time *out of the country* does count. In fact, the last 364 days of your time out of the country (1 year minus 1 day) counts toward meeting your continuous residence requirement.

You may file Form N-400 ninety (90) calendar days before you complete your permanent residence requirement if your eligibility for naturalization is based upon being a:
- Permanent resident for at least 5 years; or
- Permanent resident for at least 3 years if you are married to a U.S. citizen.

To determine your 90-day early filing date, begin by identifying your 5-year or 3-year date as a permanent resident. For example, if the date on your Permanent Resident Card says "July 4, 2006," you meet the 5 year permanent resident requirement on "July 4, 2011." If you have met all other eligibility requirements, you may file your completed Form N-400 90 days before "July 4, 2011." The earliest date you may apply for naturalization would be "April 5, 2011."

Locate the USCIS Early Filing Calculator on the USCIS website at www.uscis.gov/n-400. The calculator will help you verify that you file your Form N-400 with USCIS no more than 90 days prior to your permanent resident anniversary date. USCIS will deny your Form N-400 if you file your Form N-400 more than 90 days prior to your anniversary date.

The continuous residence requirement does not apply to certain types of applicants, such as members of the U.S. Armed Forces serving during designated periods of conflict.

Other provisions allow a few other types of applicants to remain abroad more than 1 year without disrupting their continuous residence status. To maintain their continuous residence while out of the country, these people must file an "Application to Preserve Residence for Naturalization Purposes" (Form N-470). See the table at the beginning of this section for more information on who can use Form N-470 and when it must be filed.

Physical Presence in the United States

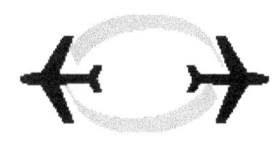

"Physical presence" means that you have actually been in the United States. Most applicants must be physically present in the United States for a certain number of months to be eligible for naturalization.

What is the difference between "physical presence" and "continuous residence"? Physical presence concerns the total number of days you were in the United States during the period required for your naturalization. Continuous residence concerns the time you resided lawfully in the United States without any single absence long enough to "break" that continuity for naturalization purposes.

"Continuous Residence" Example

- An applicant became a Permanent Resident on January 1, 1994.

- She lived in the United States for 3 years, then returned to her native country for 1 year and 3 months.

- She got a Re-entry Permit before leaving the United States so that she could keep her Permanent Resident status.

- The applicant re-entered the United States with Permanent Resident status on April 1, 1998.

Question: When is the applicant eligible for naturalization?

Answer: On April 2, 2002, 4 years and 1 day after she returned to the United States. The last 364 days the applicant was out of the United States count toward her time as a Permanent Resident in "continuous residence," but the 3 years in the United States before leaving do not.

When counting the total number of days you have been out of the country, include all trips you have taken outside the United States. This includes short trips and visits to Canada and Mexico. For example, if you go to Canada for a weekend, you must include that trip when you are counting how many days you have spent out of the country. Generally, partial days spent in the United States count as whole days spent in the United States.

Certain types of applicants may count time abroad as time physically present in the United States. An example of this exception is an applicant who is abroad in the employment of the U.S. Government. See the table at the beginning of this section for more information.

Effect of Removal Proceedings

If you have been ordered removed, you are no longer eligible for naturalization. Your naturalization application also cannot be approved if a removal proceeding is pending against you. These restrictions apply to all naturalization applicants, except for those who are eligible for naturalization based on service in the Armed Forces.

Time as a Resident in a USCIS District or State

Most people must live in the USCIS district or State in which they are applying for at least 3 months before applying. A district is a geographical area defined by USCIS and served by one of the USCIS "District Offices."

Students may apply for naturalization either where they go to school or where their family lives (if they are still financially dependent on their parents).

Important Information for Military Personnel

If you are applying for naturalization based on your own service in the Armed Forces of the United States, you may be eligible to apply under special provisions provided for in the Immigration and Nationality Act. For more information, request "Naturalization Information for Military Personnel" (Form M-599) from the USCIS Forms Line at 1-800-870-3676.

Good Moral Character

To be eligible for naturalization you must be a person of good moral character. USCIS will make a determination on your moral character based upon the laws Congress has passed. In the following section, we describe some of the things USCIS may consider.

Criminal Record. Committing certain crimes may cause you to be ineligible for naturalization (USCIS calls these "bars" to naturalization). You cannot establish that you are a person of good moral character if you have been convicted of murder, at any time, or of any other aggravated felony, if you were convicted on or after November 29, 1990.

Other offenses may be temporary bars to naturalization. Temporary bars prevent an applicant from qualifying for citizenship for a certain period of time after the offense.

The "Application for Naturalization" (Form N-400) asks several questions about crimes. You should report all offenses that you have committed including any that have been expunged (removed from your record) and any that happened before your 18th birthday. If you do not tell USCIS about these offenses and we find out about them, you may be denied naturalization (even if the original offense was not a crime for which your case would have been denied).

If you have been arrested or convicted of a crime, you must send a certified copy of the arrest report, court disposition, sentencing, and any other relevant documents, including any countervailing evidence concerning the circumstances of your arrest and/or conviction that you would like USCIS to consider. Note that unless a traffic incident was alcohol or drug related, you do not need to submit documentation for traffic fines and incidents that did not involve an actual arrest if the only penalty was a fine of less than $500 and/or points on your driver's license.

Please note that if you have committed certain serious crimes, USCIS may decide to remove you from the United States. If you have questions, you may want to seek advice from an immigrant assistance organization or an immigration attorney before applying.

Lying. If you do not tell the truth during your interview, USCIS will deny your application for lacking good moral character. If USCIS grants you naturalization and you are later found to have lied during your interview, your citizenship may be taken away.

Examples of Things That Might Demonstrate a Lack of Good Moral Character

- Any crime against a person with intent to harm.
- Any crime against property or the Government that involves "fraud" or evil intent.
- Two or more crimes for which the aggregate sentence was 5 years or more.
- Violating any controlled substance law of the United States, any State, or any foreign country.
- Habitual drunkenness.
- Illegal gambling.
- Prostitution.
- Polygamy (marriage to more than one person at the same time).
- Lying to gain immigration benefits.
- Failing to pay court-ordered child support or alimony payments.
- Confinement in jail, prison, or similar institution for which the total confinement was 180 days or more during the past 5 years (or 3 years if you are applying based on your marriage to a United States citizen).
- Failing to complete any probation, parole, or suspended sentence before you apply for naturalization.
- Terrorist acts.
- Persecution of anyone because of race, religion, national origin, political opinion, or social group.

English and Civics

According to the law, applicants must demonstrate:

- "An understanding of the English language, including an ability to read, write, and speak...simple words and phrases...in ordinary usage in the English language...."

- "A knowledge and understanding of the fundamentals of the history, and of the principles and form of government, of the United States...."

This means that to be eligible for naturalization, you must be able to read, write, and speak basic English. You must also have a basic knowledge of U.S. history and government (also known as "civics").

What if I cannot meet the English or civics requirements? Certain applicants, because of age and time as a permanent resident; or others because of a disability, have different English and civics requirements.

Age — There are three important exemptions for English testing based on an applicant's age and time as a Permanent Resident:

(a) If you are over 50 years old and have lived in the United States as a Permanent Resident for periods totaling at least 20 years, you do not have to take the English test. You do have to take the civics test in the language of your choice.

(b) If you are over 55 years old and have lived in the United States as a Permanent Resident for periods totaling at least 15 years, you do not have to take the English test. You do have to take the civics test in the language of your choice.

(c) If you are over 65 years old and have lived in the United States as a Permanent Resident for periods totaling at least 20 years, you do not have to take the English test. You do have to take the civics test in the language of your choice. Designated test questions have been selected for you to study and are identified within the list of 100 civics test questions, which can be found at **www.uscis.gov** under Education and Resources.

To qualify for one of these exceptions, your time as a Permanent Resident does not have to be continuous. You are eligible for the exemption as long as your total time residing in the United States (as a Permanent Resident) is at least 15 or 20 years. You may not count time when you were not a Permanent Resident.

You must meet these requirements for age and time as a Permanent Resident at the time you file your application to qualify for an exemption.

If you qualify for an exemption of English testing based on age and time as a Permanent Resident, an interpreter, who is proficient in English and the language of your choice, must accompany you to the interview.

Disability — If you have a physical or developmental disability or a mental impairment so severe that it prevents you from acquiring or demonstrating the required knowledge of English and civics, you may be eligible for an exception to these requirements. To request an exception, you must file a "Medical Certification for Disability Exceptions" (Form N-648). If you believe you qualify, contact a licensed medical or osteopathic doctor or licensed clinical psychologist who will need to complete and sign your Form N-648.

To apply for a disability exception, your disability:

- Must be at least 1 year old (or be expected to last 1 year); and

- Must not have been caused by illegal drug use.

If you qualify for this exception, an interpreter, who is proficient in English and the language of your choice, must accompany you to the interview.

If you qualify for a medical exception from the English and civics requirement, you must still be able to take the Oath of Allegiance to the United States. If you cannot communicate an understanding of the meaning of the oath because of a physical or mental disability, USCIS may excuse you from this requirement.

Disability Accommodations — Under section 504 of the Rehabilitation Act of 1973, USCIS provides accommodations or modifications for applicants with physical or mental impairments that make it difficult for them to complete the naturalization process. In order for USCIS to have enough advance notice to respond to accommodation requests, applicants are encouraged to state their needs on the place provided in the "Application for Naturalization" (Form N-400).

How can I prepare for the English and civics tests? Many schools and community organizations help people prepare for their naturalization tests.

USCIS has a variety of study materials available for the naturalization test at **www.uscis.gov**. These materials include the 100 civics (history and government) questions and answers; reading and writing vocabulary lists; Civics Flash Cards; and the study booklet, *Learn About the United States: Quick Civics Lessons*. In addition, you can find links to other Internet sites that can help you get more information on U.S. history and government and help you find English classes in your area.

A Guide to Naturalization

Attachment to the Constitution

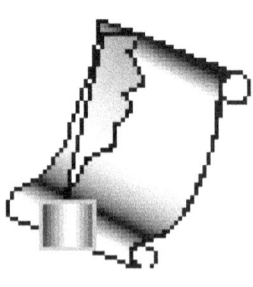

All applicants for naturalization must be willing to support and defend the United States and our Constitution. You declare your "attachment" to the United States and our Constitution when you take the Oath of Allegiance. In fact, it is not until you take the Oath of Allegiance that you actually become a U.S. citizen. If you are unwilling or unable to take the Oath of Allegiance in its entirety please see Page 38 for more information.

What does the Oath require? When you take the oath, you must promise to do three things:

The Oath of Allegiance

I hereby declare, on oath,

that I absolutely and entirely renounce and abjure all allegiance and fidelity to any foreign prince, potentate, state, or sovereignty, of whom or which I have heretofore been a subject or citizen;

that I will support and defend the Constitution and laws of the United States of America against all enemies, foreign and domestic;

that I will bear true faith and allegiance to the same;

that I will bear arms on behalf of the United States when required by the law;

that I will perform noncombatant service in the Armed Forces of the United States when required by the law;

that I will perform work of national importance under civilian direction when required by the law; and that I take this obligation freely without any mental reservation or purpose of evasion; so help me God.

---

(1) Renounce Foreign Allegiances. As stated in the oath, you must renounce all foreign allegiances to become a U.S. citizen.

(2) Support the Constitution. You must also be willing to support and defend the principles of the Constitution and the laws of the United States.

(3) Serve the United States. When required by law, you must be willing to (a) fight in the U.S. Armed Forces, (b) perform noncombatant service in the U.S. Armed Forces, and (c) perform civilian service for the United States.

What else will USCIS consider about my promise to serve the United States? In addition to your promise to serve the United States when required, USCIS also considers the following three things when determining if you are truly willing to serve the United States:

(1) *Selective Service* — If you are male, you generally need to register with the Selective Service System before applying for naturalization. If you are male and lived in the United States (in any status other than as a lawful nonimmigrant) during ages 18 through 25, you must be registered with the Selective Service System. If you are male and entered the United States after you turned 26 years old, you do not have to register with the Selective Service.

If you were required to register, you will need to provide your Selective Service number to USCIS when you apply. You may get your Selective Service number by calling **1-847-688-6888**. For men born prior to 1960, this information can be obtained by writing the Selective Service, Records Division at:

Selective Service System
National Headquarters
Arlington, VA 22209-2425

If you have not registered, you must register at a United States Post Office or on the Selective Service System's Internet site to receive a Selective Service number. The Selective Service System Internet site can be reached at **www.sss.gov** or through the USCIS Internet site at **www.uscis.gov**. You must have a Social Security number to register on the Internet.

If you were required to register, but did not register before you turned 26, you must do the following:

- Call **1-847-688-6888** or register online at **www.sss.gov** and complete the Selective Service System's Questionnaire Form. Note that registering online may speed up the process;

- Receive a "status information" letter from the Selective Service; and

- Send the "status information" letter with your application.

(2) *Alien Discharge from the U.S. Armed Forces* — If you ever received an exemption or discharge from the U.S. Armed Forces because you are an alien, you may not be eligible for naturalization.

(3) *Desertion from the U.S. Armed Forces* — If you were ever convicted of desertion from the U.S. Armed Forces, you are not eligible for naturalization. Desertion means that you left military service before you were discharged.

This page is intentionally left blank.

What Should I Expect From the Naturalization Process?

Preparing to Apply

- Read *A Guide to Naturalization*.
- Complete the Naturalization Eligibility Worksheet.
- Get an "Application for Naturalization" (Form N-400).
- Visit our website at **www.uscis.gov**.

Completing Your Application and Getting Photographed

- Complete your application.
- Get two passport-style photographs taken.
- Collect the necessary documents.
- Send your application, passport-style photographs, documents, and fee (DO NOT SEND CASH) to the appropriate Lockbox Facility or Service Center.
- Keep a copy of everything you send to USCIS.

Getting Fingerprinted

- Receive an appointment letter from USCIS.
- Go to the fingerprinting location.
- Get your fingerprints taken.
- Mail additional documents if USCIS requests them.
- Wait for USCIS to schedule your interview.

Being Interviewed

- Receive an appointment for your interview.
- Go to your local USCIS office at the specified time.
- Bring state-issued identification, Permanent Resident Card, and any additional documents specific to your case.
- Answer questions about your application and background.
- Take the English and civics tests.
- Receive case status.

Taking the Oath

- Receive a ceremony date.
- Check in at the ceremony.
- Return your Permanent Resident Card.
- Answer questions about what you have done since your interview.
- Take the Oath of Allegiance.
- Receive your Certificate of Naturalization.

Preparing to Apply

1. Read *A Guide to Naturalization*

Reading *A Guide to Naturalization* is the first step in the naturalization process. We realize that some naturalization requirements may be difficult to understand. If you read this *Guide* before beginning the naturalization process, many of your questions will be answered.

We hope that the information in this *Guide* will help you prepare your application. If you are well prepared, and send us the necessary information and documents, we can process your application more quickly. It is your responsibility to begin the naturalization process fully informed and ready to provide the necessary information and documents.

2. Complete the Naturalization Eligibility Worksheet

Complete the Eligibility Worksheet in the back of this *Guide* to decide if you are eligible to apply for naturalization. If you do not meet all the requirements, you may save both time and money by waiting until you are eligible to apply.

If you complete the Eligibility Worksheet and have questions about your eligibility, you should seek advice by:

- Calling Customer Service at **1-800-375-5283**;

- Reviewing the information on the USCIS website at **www.uscis.gov**;

- Going to a USCIS information counter;

- Contacting a community immigrant assistance organization; or

- Talking to an immigration attorney.

3. Get an "Application for Naturalization" (Form N-400)

Once you have completed the eligibility worksheet and believe that you are eligible for naturalization, you should obtain an application. The application is called the "Application for Naturalization" (Form N-400). You may obtain Form N-400 by calling the USCIS Forms Line **(1-800-870-3676)** or by downloading it from the Internet at **www.uscis.gov**.

USCIS has developed educational materials, such as Civics Flash Cards and *Learn About the United States: Quick Civics Lessons*, to help you prepare for the naturalization interview. You can find these resources and other study materials for the naturalization test at **www.uscis.gov**.

Completing Your Application and Getting Photographed

1. Complete your application

Once you have Form N-400, you must fill it out completely. USCIS may ask for additional information if your application is incomplete. This will delay the processing of your naturalization application.

You will be required to answer questions about your application at your interview. When completing your application, you should answer all questions honestly. Be sure to keep a copy of your completed application for your records.

2. Get two photographs taken

You must include two standard, passport-style, color photographs with your application.

Be sure there is enough white space in the margin of the photographs so you will have room to sign your full name if your application is approved. The photographs must also be:

- Unmounted and printed on thin paper, on a white background with a full frontal view of your face; and

- Taken within 30 days of the date they are sent to USCIS.

Finally, your head should be bare (unless you are required by your religious beliefs to wear a headcovering). In all cases, your facial features must be visible.

You should print your name and "A–number" lightly in pencil on the back of each photograph. For more information on photograph requirements, see the single page titled "USCIS is Making Photos Simpler," at **www.uscis.gov**.

For more information on photo standards, visit the Department of State's website at **www.travel.state.gov** or contact Customer Service at **1-800-375-5283**.

3. Collect the necessary documents

Applicants who are lawful permanent residents of the United States must submit photocopies (front and back) of Form I-551 (Permanent Resident Card). Depending on the circumstances, some applicants must send certain documents with their application. For more information on the documents you must send with your application, see the Document Checklist located at the back of this *Guide*. If you do not send the necessary documents with your application, the processing of your application may be delayed. In most cases, you should send a copy of a document, but you should be prepared to bring the originals with you to your interview. We may also ask you to send other documents to us before your interview, or to bring additional documents with you to your interview.

Be sure to send an English translation with any document that is not already in English. The translation must include a statement from the translator that he or she is competent to translate and that the translation is correct.

If you do not have a required document and cannot get a certified copy of the original, submit a certification from the original recording authority explaining why it cannot be provided. In that case we will consider other evidence such as notarized affidavits.

The Document Checklist will tell you when you need to send original documents and when you may send copies. Remember to make and keep copies of all documents you send to USCIS.

A Guide to Naturalization

4. Send your application, documents, and fee to the USCIS Lockbox Facility

Send your application directly to the USCIS Lockbox that serves your area. If you try to take or mail your application to a local USCIS office, it will be returned to you.

The current fee you must send with your application is on the one-page insert titled "Current Naturalization Fees" in the back of this *Guide*. Military applicants filing for citizenship under Sections 328 and 329 of the INA do not require a fee.

If you reside in Alaska, Arizona, California, Colorado, Hawaii, Idaho, Illinois, Indiana, Iowa, Kansas, Michigan, Minnesota, Missouri, Montana, Nebraska, Nevada, North Dakota, Ohio, Oregon, South Dakota, Utah, Washington, Wisconsin, Wyoming, Territory of Guam, or Northern Mariana Islands, send your application to:

USCIS Lockbox Facility
USCIS
P.O. Box 21251
Phoenix, AZ 85036

Private Courier (non-USPS) Deliveries:
USCIS
Attention: N-400
1820 E. Skyharbor Circle S.
Suite 100
Phoenix, AZ 85034

If you reside in Alabama, Arkansas, Connecticut, Delaware, District of Columbia, Florida, Georgia, Kentucky, Louisiana, Maine, Maryland, Massachusetts, Mississippi, New Hampshire, New Jersey, New Mexico, New York, North Carolina, Oklahoma, Pennsylvania, Puerto Rico, Rhode Island, South Carolina, Tennessee, Texas, Vermont, Virginia, West Virginia, or U.S. Virgin Islands, send your application to:

USCIS Lockbox Facility
USCIS
P.O. Box 660060
Dallas, TX 75266

Private Courier (non-USPS) Deliveries:
USCIS
Attention: N-400
2501 S. State Hwy 121 Business
Suite 400
Lewisville, TX 75067

Military Members and Spouses: If you are a veteran or an active member of the U.S. Armed Forces and are eligible to apply for naturalization under Section 328 or 329 of the INA, **or are the spouse of a current member of the U.S. Armed Forces**, send your application to:

USCIS Service Center
Nebraska Service Center
P.O. Box 87426
Lincoln, NE 68501-7426

Private Courier (non-USPS) Deliveries:
Nebraska Service Center
850 S Street
Lincoln, NE 68508

What if I live overseas? If you are overseas and filing Form N-400, you should send your application to the USCIS Lockbox Facility that serves the USCIS office where you want to be interviewed.

What if I am currently serving in active duty status in the military? If you are applying for naturalization based on qualifying military service, and are currently serving in an active duty status, you may go to your service's personnel office for information on how to prepare your application. You should speak to your personnel office even if you are stationed overseas. For more information, see "Naturalization Information for Military Personnel" (Form M-599).

Getting Fingerprinted

1. Receive an appointment letter from USCIS

Once you have filed your application, USCIS will send you a letter telling you where and when to have your fingerprints taken.

In most cases, the letter will tell you to go to an Application Support Center. A van may be available in certain areas of Alaska and Hawaii to fingerprint applicants who are located far from the nearest fingerprinting location. Your notice from USCIS will tell you if a van serves your area.

2. Go to the fingerprinting location

Take your notice letter from USCIS, your Permanent Resident Card, and another form of identification (driver's license, passport, or State identification card) with you. Your second form of identification should have your photograph on it.

If you are 75 years or older at the time you file your application, you do not have to be fingerprinted. If you are living overseas, USCIS will tell you to have your fingerprints taken at a U.S. consular office.

3. Get your fingerprints taken

Currently, all sites take fingerprints electronically. However, manual workstations are available for applicants whose prints cannot be taken electronically.

In order to do a criminal background check, USCIS will send your fingerprints to the Federal Bureau of Investigation (FBI). In some cases, the FBI may reject your fingerprints because of the quality of the prints.

If the FBI rejects your fingerprints, USCIS will notify you and schedule a second visit to the fingerprinting site. You will not be asked to pay again.

If the FBI rejects your fingerprints twice, you will be asked to provide police clearances for each place you have lived in the past 5 years. You will need to contact the police departments in the places you have lived to get these clearances.

4. Mail additional documents if USCIS requests them

While the FBI is checking your background, USCIS will locate your immigration file. Sometimes USCIS may need additional documents from you before we can schedule your interview. If USCIS needs more information from you, we will send you a letter telling you what information we need and where to send it.

5. Wait for USCIS to schedule your interview

Once everything is ready, USCIS will schedule you for an interview. USCIS will send you an interview notice in the mail that will tell you the date, time, and place of your interview.

Being Interviewed

1. Receive an appointment for your interview

USCIS will send you a notice in the mail telling you when and where you must appear for your interview. You will not receive a second notice.

What if I cannot go to my interview? If you must reschedule your interview, you should write to the office where your interview is scheduled as soon as possible. You should explain your situation and ask to have your interview rescheduled. When a new date has been set, USCIS will send you a new interview notice.

To make sure you get your interview notice, you must notify USCIS every time your address changes.

2. Go to your local USCIS office at the specified time

You should go to the office where you are to be interviewed at least 30 minutes before the time of your interview. Many USCIS offices are crowded, so unless you need to, you may not want to bring other people with you to your interview.

If you do not go to your interview and do not contact USCIS beforehand, we will "administratively close" your case. If we administratively close your case and you do not contact USCIS within 1 year to reopen your case, we will deny your application.

Rescheduling an interview may add several months to the naturalization process, so try to attend your original interview date.

3. Bring identification and provide additional documents if USCIS requests them

You should bring the following identification to your interview: (a) your Permanent Resident or Alien Registration Card, (b) your passport (even if it has expired), (c) State Identification Card, and (d) any Re-entry Permits you have.

In some cases, USCIS may ask you to bring additional documents to the interview. These documents will be listed on your appointment letter. If you don't bring the necessary documents, your case may be delayed or denied. USCIS strongly recommends that you also bring two additional passport-style photographs with you to the interview.

4. Answer questions about your application and background.

At your interview, a USCIS officer will explain the purpose of the interview, ask to see your identification, and place you under oath. He or she will ask you about:

- Your background;

- Evidence supporting your case;

- Your place and length of residence;

- Your character;

- Your attachment to the Constitution; and

- Your willingness to take an Oath of Allegiance to the United States.

In addition, the USCIS officer may ask you some other questions to make sure that you meet all the eligibility requirements. Be prepared to explain any differences between your application and the other documents you provided to USCIS.

Remember that you are under oath. Always tell the truth during your interview. If you lie during your interview, you will be denied citizenship. If you are granted citizenship, but then USCIS finds out that you lied on your application or during your interview, your citizenship may be taken away.

If you want a representative to accompany you to your interview, you must first send us a "Notice of Entry of Appearance as Attorney or Representative" (Form G-28) with your application. Also, if you are exempt from the English requirements, you may bring an interpreter to the interview or USCIS may select one for you. If you have any disabilities, you may bring a family member or legal guardian to be present with you during the interview at the discretion of the USCIS officer.

5. Take the English and civics tests

During your interview, a USCIS officer will also test your ability to read, write, and speak English (unless you are exempt from the English requirements). You will also be given a civics test in English (to test your knowledge and understanding of U.S. history and government) unless you are exempt. Even if exempt from the English test, you will need to take the civics test in the language of your choice or qualify for a waiver.

English. Study materials have been publicly released by USCIS and are available at **www.uscis.gov** under Education and Resources. Your English skills will be tested in the following ways:

(1) Reading. To test your ability to read in English, you must read one sentence, out of three sentences, in a manner suggesting to the USCIS officer that you understand the meaning of the sentence.

(2) Writing. To test your ability to write in English, you must write one sentence, out of three sentences, in a manner that would be understandable as written to the USCIS officer.

(3) Speaking. Your ability to speak English is determined by your answers to questions normally asked by USCIS officers during the naturalization eligibility interview on Form N-400.

Civics. During your interview, the USCIS officer will ask you to orally answer a set of civics questions. You must answer six (6) out of 10 civics questions correctly to achieve a passing score. All 100 civics questions have been publicly released by USCIS and are available at **www.uscis.gov** under Education and Resources.

6. Receive a decision

After your interview, we will give you a Form N-652 that gives you information about the results of your interview. Based on all the information you have given us, we will either grant, continue, or deny your naturalization application after your interview.

Granted. Sometimes USCIS can tell you if you will be granted citizenship at the end of your interview. In some cases, you may be able to attend an oath ceremony the same day as your interview (where available). Otherwise, you will receive a notice telling you when and where your oath ceremony will be.

Continued. The USCIS officer may also "continue" your case. This means your case is put on hold. If your case is continued, it will add time to your naturalization process. The most common reasons for continuation are (a) failing the English and civics tests, and (b) failing to give USCIS the correct documents.

When your case is continued, you will be asked to do one of two things:

(1) Come back for a second interview. If you fail one or both of the tests, we will reschedule you to come back for another interview, usually within 60-90 days of the first interview. At that time, you will be tested again. If you fail the test(s) a second time, we will deny your application.

(2) Provide additional documents. If USCIS needs more information from you, we will give you a Form N-14. This form explains what information or documents you must provide us, and tells you when and how you should return the information to us. If you do not follow the instructions, we may deny your application.

Denied. USCIS may also deny your application for naturalization. If USCIS denies your application for naturalization, you will receive a written notice telling you why.

What can I do if USCIS denies my application? If you feel that USCIS was wrong to deny you citizenship, you may request a hearing with a USCIS officer. Your denial letter will explain how to request a hearing and will include the form you need. The form for filing an appeal is the "Request for Hearing on a Decision in Naturalization Proceedings under Section 336 of the INA" (Form N-336). You must file the form with USCIS, including the correct fee, within 30 days after you receive a denial letter.

If, after an appeal hearing with USCIS, you still believe USCIS was wrong to deny you citizenship, you may file a petition for a new review of your application in U.S. District Court.

A Guide to Naturalization

Taking the Oath

1. Receive a ceremony date

If USCIS approves your application for naturalization, you must attend a ceremony and take the Oath of Allegiance to the United States. USCIS will notify you by mail of the time and date of your ceremony.

The notice USCIS sends you is called the "Notice of Naturalization Oath Ceremony" (Form N-445). In some cases, USCIS may give you the option to take the oath on the same day as your interview.

If you arrange to take a "same-day" oath, USCIS will ask you to come back to the office later that day. At this time, you will take the oath and receive your Certificate of Naturalization.

2. Check in at the ceremony

When you arrive at the ceremony, you will be asked to check in with USCIS. You should arrive at least 30 minutes before your scheduled ceremony. Remember that there are often many other people being naturalized with you who must also be checked in with USCIS.

If you cannot attend the ceremony on the day you are scheduled, you should return the USCIS notice (Form N-445) to your local USCIS office. You should include a letter explaining why you cannot be at the ceremony and asking USCIS to reschedule you.

The naturalization ceremony is a solemn and meaningful event. Please dress in proper attire to respect the dignity of this event (please no jeans, shorts, or flip flops).

3. Return your Permanent Resident Card

You must return your Permanent Resident Card to USCIS when you check in for your oath ceremony. You will no longer need your Permanent Resident Card because you will get your Certificate of Naturalization at the ceremony.

4. Answer questions about what you have done since your interview

If more than a day has passed between your interview and the ceremony, we will ask you several questions. These questions will be on the back of the notice (Form N-445) USCIS sends you.

Some questions on the back of the N-445 include: "Have you traveled outside the United States?" and "Have you claimed exemption from military service?" You should read the questions carefully and mark your answers before you arrive at the ceremony.

Answer the questions on the back of Form N-445 only for the time since your interview.

5. Take the Oath

Every naturalization candidate is required to recite the Oath of Allegiance to become a U.S. citizen. The words of the Oath of Allegiance can be found on Page 28. The Oath of Allegiance must be recited at a formal naturalization ceremony in front of a USCIS official. Once recited, USCIS will issue you a Certificate of Naturalization.

Waiver or Modification of the Oath of Allegiance. In certain circumstances there can be a modification or waiver of the Oath of Allegiance. These circumstances are as follows:

- If you are unable or unwilling to promise to bear arms or perform noncombatant service because of religious training and belief, you may request to leave out those parts of the oath. USCIS may require you to provide documentation from your religious organization explaining its beliefs and stating that you are a member in good standing.

- If you are unable or unwilling to take the oath with the words "on oath" and "so help me God" included, you must notify USCIS that you wish to take a modified Oath of Allegiance. Applicants are not required to provide any evidence or testimony to support a request for this type of modification. See 8 CFR 337.1(b).

- USCIS can waive the Oath of Allegiance when it is shown that the person's physical or developmental disability, or mental impairments, makes them unable to understand, or to communicate an understanding of, the meaning of the oath. See 8 USC 337.

Hereditary Titles. If you have any hereditary titles or positions of nobility, you must renounce at the oath ceremony.

6. Receive your Certificate of Naturalization

Once you have taken the oath, you will receive your Certificate of Naturalization. You may use this document as proof that you are a U.S. citizen.

We strongly recommend that you go to your nearest Social Security Administration (SSA) office to update your Social Security record soon after your naturalization ceremony.

This is important because your Social Security record will be used to establish eligibility for benefits and to demonstrate authorization to work. The nearest SSA office can be found by calling 1-800-772-1213 or at **www.socialsecurity.gov**.

To Update your Citizenship with SSA. In order to update your citizenship status in your SSA record, you will need to present your Certificate of Naturalization or your U.S. passport to the SSA.

To Change your Name in SSA's Records. If at the oath ceremony you also changed your name from that shown in your SSA record, and your Certificate of Naturalization does not show your old and new names, you will also need to present:

- A State driver's license or other acceptable form of identification in your old name as shown in your SSA record. This identity document in your former name can be unexpired or expired. It must contain your photo and/or biographical information about you.

- If you changed your name more than two years ago, you will also need to present a recently issued identity document showing your new legal name as shown on your Certificate of Naturalization or U.S. passport.

- **E-Verify Program.** SSA's records will be used to verify your employment eligibility by all employers who use E-Verify. In order to prevent name-related mismatches in E-Verify, the name that you provide on your "Employment Eligibility Verification" (Form I-9) must match the name that is in SSA's records. Therefore, we encourage you to update your records with SSA as soon as possible.

Apply for a U.S. Passport. We strongly recommend that you apply for a U.S. passport soon after your oath. You will not be able to travel abroad until you have your U.S. passport. Please allow sufficient time between your ceremony and any planned travel to receive your passport.

- In addition to your Certificate of Naturalization, a passport serves as evidence of citizenship. If you lose your Certificate of Naturalization, you may request a replacement by filing an "Application for Replacement Naturalization/Citizenship Document" (Form N-565).

- You can get an application for a passport at your oath ceremony in the U.S. Citizenship Welcome Packet or at most United States Post Offices. On the web, visit http://travel.state.gov.

This page is intentionally left blank.

What Kind of Customer Service Can I Expect?

You should expect USCIS staff to be:
- Professional.
- Courteous.
- Knowledgeable.

You should expect the naturalization process to be:
- Fair.
- Consistent.
- Timely.

You should expect information on the naturalization process and on the status of your application to be:
- Accurate.
- Readily available.

USCIS also expects certain things from you. You should:
- Treat USCIS employees with courtesy.
- Read *A Guide to Naturalization*.
- Read and follow the instructions on your application.
- Be prepared at each step of the process.

Making a Customer Service Complaint

USCIS realizes that in some offices it takes a long time to process applications. We are currently working to reduce processing times. If you have a question about processing, please visit **www.uscis.gov** or call Customer Service at **1-800-375-5283 (TTY: 1-800-767-1833)**.

If you have a complaint about the way that a USCIS employee treated you, you should speak with that employee's direct supervisor if possible. If your complaint is not handled to your satisfaction, or if you could not speak with the supervisor, you may write a letter to the director of your USCIS District Office. Filing a complaint will not affect your eligibility for naturalization.

This page is intentionally left blank.

Where Do I Go for Help?

There are many resources available to naturalization applicants. Some of these are:

Customer Service. If you need more information about the naturalization process and you live in the continental United States, you may call Customer Service at no charge **(1-800-375-5283)** for help. Not all services may be available to callers from all areas.

Community-Based Organizations (CBOs). In most communities, there are organizations that assist immigrants who want to become citizens. These organizations often offer classes to prepare immigrants for the English and civics requirements. They may also help immigrants complete their applications. CBOs may charge a fee or they may offer their services free of charge.

You may locate a CBO by contacting your local USCIS office. You may also look in the phone book under "Immigration and Naturalization" or "Immigration and Naturalization Consultants" or talk to other immigrants who have been naturalized.

Adult Education Classes. In many communities, there are adult education classes to help you learn English. Some classes can teach you English and U.S. civics and history at the same time. To find these classes, you can call your local community college or public school district office. Look in the blue pages of your phone book under "Schools - Public." Some CBOs and public libraries also offer English classes.

You should be certain that the organization or attorney you contact is reliable and has a good reputation. One way to be sure of the quality of a CBO is to ask them for references or if the Board of Immigration Appeals (BIA) accredits them.

USCIS Internet Site. You can learn more about immigration and naturalization, download relevant forms, including Form N-400, and *A Guide to Naturalization*, and get other information, including educational materials to help you prepare for the English and civics tests, from the USCIS website at **www.uscis.gov**.

Immigration Attorneys. If you have questions about your eligibility for naturalization, you may want to talk to an immigration attorney. Attorneys are usually listed in the phone book under "Lawyers" or "Attorneys." In many cases, the phone book also has a directory of attorneys by the type of law they practice. You may be able to find attorneys who assist immigrants by looking in the directory under "Immigration and Naturalization."

USCIS Information Counters. If you have questions that have not been answered either by this *Guide* or by the other resources listed here, you may always go to the information counter at your local USCIS office. There you may speak directly to a USCIS representative. To make an appointment at your local USCIS office, visit our website at **www.uscis.gov** and click on InfoPass.

A Guide to Naturalization

This page is intentionally left blank.

Glossary of Terms

A Guide to Naturalization – The booklet you are reading.

Aggravated Felony – Usually refers to particularly serious crimes. If you have committed an aggravated felony, you may be permanently ineligible for naturalization. The Immigration and Nationality Act and the laws in each State determine what is considered an aggravated felony.

Application Support Center (ASC) – USCIS offices where applicants usually have their fingerprints taken. Once you have filed your application with USCIS, you will receive a notice telling you which ASC serves your area.

AR-11, "Alien's Change of Address Card" – This is the form you use to tell USCIS when you have moved to a new address. The AR-11 is pre-printed with USCIS' address. It is very important to tell USCIS when your address changes. This way, you will receive any information USCIS sends you, including interview notices and requests for additional documents.

Certificate of Naturalization – A certificate given at the oath ceremony. It serves as evidence of your citizenship. USCIS also recommends getting a United States passport as evidence that you are a U.S. citizen.

Community-Based Organization (CBO) – Organizations that assist immigrants who are new to the United States or who are going through the naturalization process. Many CBOs will help you complete your application and guide you through the naturalization process. CBOs may charge a fee or offer their services free of charge.

Constitution – The supreme law of the United States. It may be changed only through amendment by Congress and ratification by three-fourths of the States.

Continued – One of three things that may happen to your case after your interview (granted, denied, or continued). If your case is continued, it is put on hold until further action is taken by you or USCIS. If your case is continued, USCIS may ask you to provide more documents or to come to an additional interview.

Continuous Residence – An important requirement for naturalization. Continuous residence may be broken if you take a single trip out of the country that lasts for 6 months or more.

Denied – One of three things that may happen to your case after your interview (granted, denied, or continued). If your application is denied, USCIS has determined that you have not met the eligibility requirements for naturalization.

Districts – The geographic divisions of the United States used by USCIS.

G-28, "Notice of Entry of Appearance as Attorney or Representative" – The form you must file with your Form N-400 if you wish to bring a representative with you to your USCIS interview.

Good Moral Character – Good moral character is an important eligibility requirement for naturalization. When determining if an applicant has good moral character, USCIS considers such things as honesty and criminal records.

Granted – One of three things that may happen to your case after your interview (granted, denied, or continued). If USCIS determines that you are eligible, your application will be approved or "granted." After you take the Oath of Allegiance, you will be a United States citizen.

N-400, "Application for Naturalization" – The N-400 is the form that all people 18 years of age or older use to apply for naturalization.

N-445, "Notice of Naturalization Oath Ceremony" – If you are approved for naturalization, you will receive an N-445 telling you when and where to attend your oath ceremony. On the back of the form will be several questions that you must answer before you check in at the ceremony.

N-470, "Application to Preserve Residence for Naturalization Purposes" – The N-470 is a form that certain types of applicants who plan to remain longer than a year outside the United States may file to preserve "continuous residence" status.

N-565, "Application for Replacement Naturalization/ Citizenship Document" – If you lose your Certificate of Naturalization, or your Certificate of Citizenship, you may file an N-565 to get a replacement. USCIS advises naturalized citizens to also obtain a United States passport as evidence of their U.S. citizenship.

N-600, "Application for Certificate of Citizenship" – Qualified U.S. residents born outside the United States to U.S. citizen parents, or parents who became citizens, may file a Form N-600 to get a Certificate of Citizenship.

N-600K, "Application for Citizenship and Issuance of Certificate under Section 322" – Qualified children born to U.S. citizen parents, and currently residing outside the United States, may obtain naturalization and a Certificate of Citizenship by filing Form N-600K.

N-648, "Medical Certification for Disability Exceptions" – The form used to apply for a disability exemption. If you have a qualifying medical disability that prevents you from fulfilling the English and civics requirement, you must have a licensed medical or osteopathic doctor, or licensed clinical psychologist complete and sign an N-648. Applicants are encouraged, but not required, to submit the N-648 at the time of filing the N-400 to ensure timely adjudication of both applications.

Naturalization – Naturalization is the process by which immigrants apply to become U.S. citizens.

Naturalization Eligibility Worksheet – This is a worksheet in the back of this *Guide* that you may use as a tool to determine whether you are eligible for naturalization. Do not send this worksheet to USCIS at any time; it is for your use only.

Oath Ceremony – To become a naturalized citizen of the United States, you must attend an oath ceremony where you take the Oath of Allegiance to the United States.

Oath of Allegiance to the United States – The oath you take to become a U.S. citizen. When you take the Oath of Allegiance to the United States, you are promising to give up your allegiance to other countries and to support and defend the United States and its Constitution and laws. Ability to take and understand the Oath of Allegiance is a normal requirement for becoming a naturalized U.S. citizen.

Outlying Possessions – The current outlying possessions of the United States are American Samoa and Swains Island.

Permanent Resident – A Permanent Resident is a person who has been granted permanent resident status in the United States and has (or is waiting for) a Permanent Resident Card.

Permanent Resident Card – The Permanent Resident Card is a USCIS document that identifies a person as a Permanent Resident. The Permanent Resident Card may be identified as Form I-551. The Permanent Resident Card used to be known as the Alien Registration Card and/or "Green Card."

Physical Presence – Physical presence in the United States is an important eligibility requirement. Most naturalization applicants must spend a specified amount of time in the United States in order to meet the physical presence requirement for naturalization.

Except in a few cases, time spent outside of the United States, even brief trips to Canada and Mexico, does not count toward your "physical presence."

Port-of-Entry – The Port-of-Entry is the place where you legally entered the country as a Permanent Resident.

Selective Service – The Selective Service System is the Federal agency responsible for providing manpower to the U.S. Armed Forces in an emergency. Male applicants generally are required to have registered with the Selective Service before applying for naturalization. See pages 28-29 for information on who is required to register, how to register, and what to do if you were required to register but did not, or call the Selective Service System at **1-847-688-6888** for more information.

Service Center – USCIS Service Centers handle and adjudicate most applications for immigration services and benefits. There are four USCIS Service Centers in the United States.

USCIS Forms Line – The USCIS Forms Line distributes all forms for immigration and naturalization. You can call the Forms Line at **1-800-870-3676** to have any USCIS forms sent to you, including the "Application for Naturalization" (Form N-400).

USCIS Information Counter – USCIS offices have information counters staffed by USCIS employees called Immigration Information Officers (IIOs). IIOs are available to answer questions you have about naturalization. Remember to use InfoPass to make an appointment to talk to an IIO. Visit our website at **www.uscis.gov** for instructions on how to use InfoPass.

USCIS Lockbox Facility – There are four Lockbox Facilities in the United States that handle the receipting of applications for immigration services and benefits.

U.S. National (but not U.S. Citizen) – A person who, because of his or her birth in American Samoa or on Swains Island, owes permanent allegiance to the United States, and who may naturalize based on residence in an outlying possession of the United States.

United States Passport – A U.S. passport is an official document that identifies you as a U.S. citizen. All naturalized citizens are encouraged to get a passport as soon as possible after they are naturalized.

Department of Homeland Security
U.S. Citizenship and Immigration Services

M-477

Document Checklist

All applicants must send the following 3 items with their N-400 application:

1. ☐ A photocopy of both sides of your Permanent Resident Card (formerly known as the Alien Registration Card or "Green Card"). If you have lost the card, submit a photocopy of the receipt of your Form I-90, Application to Replace Permanent Resident Card; **and**

2. ☐ **2** identical color photographs, with your name and Alien Registration Number (A-Number) written lightly in pencil on the back of each photo. For details about the photo requirements, see **Part 5** of Form M-476, A Guide to Naturalization, and the Form N-400, Application for Naturalization instructions. If your religion requires you to wear a head covering, your facial features must still be exposed in the photo for purposes of identification; **and**

3. ☐ A check or money order for the application fee and the biometrics services fee for fingerprinting, as stated in the M-479, Current Naturalization Fees, enclosure in the *Guide*. (Applicants 75 years of age or older are exempted from fingerprinting and the biometrics services fee). Write your A-Number on the back of the check or money order.

Send copies of the following documents, unless we ask for an original.

If an attorney or accredited representative is acting on your behalf, send:
☐ A completed original Form G-28, Notice of Entry of Appearance as Attorney or Representative.

If your current legal name is different from the name on your Permanent Resident Card, send:
☐ The document(s) that legally changed your name (marriage certificate, divorce decree, or court document).

If you are applying for naturalization on the basis of marriage to a U.S. citizen, send the following 4 items:

1. ☐ Evidence that your spouse has been a U.S. citizen for the last 3 years:
   a. Birth certificate (if your spouse never lost citizenship since birth); **or**
   b. Certificate of Naturalization; **or**
   c. Certificate of Citizenship; **or**
   d. The inside of the front cover and signature page of your spouse's current U.S. passport; **or**
   e. Form FS-240, Report of Birth Abroad of a Citizen of the United States of America; **and**
2. ☐ Your current marriage certificate; **and**
3. ☐ Proof of termination of all prior marriages of your spouse (divorce decree(s), annulment(s), or death certificate(s)); **and**
4. ☐ Documents referring to you and your spouse:
   a. Tax returns, bank accounts, leases, mortgages, or birth certificates of children; **or**
   b. Internal Revenue Service (IRS)-certified copies of the income tax forms that you both filed for the past 3 years; **or**
   c. An IRS tax return transcript for the last 3 years.

If you were married before, send:
☐ Proof that **all** earlier marriages ended (divorce decree(s), annulment(s), or death certificates(s)).

If you are currently in the U.S. military service and are seeking citizenship based on that service, send:
☐ A completed original Form N-426, Request for Certification of Military or Naval Service.

If you have taken any trip outside the United States that lasted 6 months or more since becoming a Lawful Permanent Resident, send evidence that you (and your family) continued to live, work and/or keep ties to the United States, such as:
☐ An IRS tax return "transcript" or an IRS-certified tax return listing tax information for the last 5 years (or for the last 3 years if you are applying on the basis of marriage to a U.S. citizen).
☐ Rent or mortgage payments and pay stubs.

Form M-477 (Rev. 02/10/2011 N)

If you have a dependent spouse or child(ren) who do not live with you, send:
- [ ] Any court or government order to provide financial support; **and**
- [ ] Evidence of your financial support (including evidence that you have complied with any court or government order), such as:
    a. Cancelled checks;
    b. Money and receipts;
    c. A court or agency printout of child support payments;
    d. Evidence of wage garnishments;
    e. A letter from the parent or guardian who cares for your child(ren).

If you have ever been arrested or detained by any law enforcement officer for any reason, and <u>no charges were filed</u>, send:
- [ ] An <u>original</u> official statement by the arresting agency or applicant court confirming that no charges were filed.

If you have ever been arrested or detained by any law enforcement officer for any reason, and <u>charges were filed</u>, send:
- [ ] An <u>original</u> or court-certified copy of the complete arrest record and disposition for each incident (dismissal order, conviction record **or** acquittal order).

If you have ever been convicted or placed in an alternative sentencing program or rehabilitative program (such as a drug treatment or community service program), send:
- [ ] An <u>original</u> or court-certified copy of the sentencing record for each incident; **and**
- [ ] Evidence that you completed your sentence:
    a. An <u>original</u> or certified copy of your probation or parole record; **or**
    b. Evidence that you completed an alternative sentencing program or rehabilitative program.

If you have ever had any arrest or conviction vacated, set aside, sealed, expunged or otherwise removed from your record, send:
- [ ] An <u>original</u> or court-certified copy of the court order vacating, setting aside, sealing, expunging or otherwise removing the arrest or conviction, **or** an <u>original</u> statement from the court that no record exists of your arrest or conviction.

    NOTE: If you have been arrested or convicted of a crime, you may send any countervailing evidence or evidence in your favor concerning the circumstances of your arrest and/or conviction that you would like U.S. Citizenship and Immigration Services to consider.

If you have ever failed to file an income tax return since you became a Lawful Permanent Resident, send:
- [ ] All correspondence with the IRS regarding your failure to file.

If you have any Federal, state or local taxes that are overdue, send:
- [ ] A signed agreement from the IRS or state or local tax office showing that you have filed a tax return and arranged to pay the taxes you owe; **and**
- [ ] Documentation from the IRS or state or local tax office showing the current status of your repayment program.

    NOTE: You may obtain copies of tax documents and tax information by contacting your local IRS offices, using the Blue Pages of your telephone directory, or through its Web site at **www.irs.gov**.

If you are applying for a disability exception to the testing requirement, send:
- [ ] An <u>original</u> Form N-648, Medical Certification for Disability Exceptions, completed less than 6 months ago by a licensed medical or osteopathic doctor or licensed clinical psychologist.

If you did not register with the Selective Service and you (1) are male, (2) are 26 years old or older, and (3) lived in the United States in a status other than as a lawful nonimmigrant between the ages of 18 and 26, send:
- [ ] A "Status Information Letter" from the Selective Service (Call **1-847-688-6888** for more information).

Department of Homeland Security
U.S. Citizenship and Immigration Services

M-479

Current Naturalization Fees

The fee for filing your naturalization application is:* $595.00

The biometric services fee for having your fingerprints taken is:** $ 85.00

Total: $680.00

You must send the **$680.00** fee with your application. Pay the fee with a check or money order drawn on a U.S. bank payable to the **Department of Homeland Security**. Do not use the initials DHS or USDHS. **Do Not Send Cash.**

Residents of Guam should make the fee payable to the "Treasurer, Guam," and residents of the U.S. Virgin Islands should make the fee payable to the "Commissioner of Finance of the Virgin Islands."

If required, USCIS may also take your photograph and signature as part of the biometric services.

Remember that your application fee is not refundable even if you withdraw your application or if your case is denied.

* If you are applying for naturalization based on your own service in the Armed Forces of the United States, no filing fee is required.

** If you are 75 years or older, or if you are filing on the basis of your service in the Armed Forces of the United States, or if you are filing from abroad, **do not** send the biometric services fee for fingerprinting with your application.

Department of Homeland Security
U.S. Citizenship and Immigration Services

M-480

Naturalization Eligibility Worksheet Instructions

What Is the Purpose of This Worksheet?
The attached "Eligibility Worksheet" will help you decide if you are eligible to apply for naturalization. **Do not send the completed worksheet to U.S. Citizenship and Immigration Services (USCIS).**

Who Should Complete This Worksheet?
If you are 18 years of age or older and are thinking about applying for naturalization based on your years as a Permanent Resident, you should complete this worksheet.

Who Should Not Use This Worksheet?
You **should not** use this worksheet to decide your eligibilty to apply if you are:

- Under 18 years of age and want to apply for naturalization based on your parents' or adopted parents' citizenship (see Questions 25 and 26 on pages 13-15 in *A Guide to Naturalization* for information on how to obtain citizenship).

- A Permanent Resident whose spouse was a U.S. citizen who died while on active duty in the U.S. Armed Forces (see pages 18 and 19 in *A Guide to Naturalization* for information on your naturalization requirements).

- Applying for naturalization based on active duty service in the U.S. Armed Forces (see pages 18 and 19 in *A Guide to Naturalization* for information on your naturalization requirements).

- A spouse of a U.S. citizen who is (a) a member of the U.S. Armed Forces, (b) an employee or contractor of the U.S. Government, (c) an employee of an American institution of research, (d) an employee of an American owned firm, (e) an employee of a public international organization, or (f) a clergy member (see pages 20 and 21 in *A Guide to Naturalization* for more information).

Directions for the Eligibility Worksheet:

1. Answer the questions on the worksheet by checking "True" or "Not True." If you answer "Not True" to certain questions, you may be asked to answer additional questions on pages 3 and 4. Most applicants will **not** need to answer the questions on pages 3 and 4.

2. If you have completed the worksheet and believe you are eligible for naturalization, please call the USCIS Forms Line **(1-800-870-3676)** to request an application (Form N-400), or download the form from the Internet at **www.uscis.gov.**

3. If you have completed the worksheet and you still have questions regarding your eligibility, you should read *A Guide to Naturalization.* You may also wish to get advice from an immigrant assistance organization or immigration attorney.

Naturalization Eligibility Worksheet

	True	Not True	
1. I am at least 18 years old.	☐	☐ STOP →	You are not eligible to apply for naturalization. **Exception:** You do not need to be at least 18 years old for military naturalization under section 329 of the INA.
2. I am a Permanent Resident of the United States, and I have been issued a Permanent Resident Card (formerly called Alien Registration Card).	☐	☐ STOP →	You are not eligible to apply for naturalization.

3. I have been a Permanent Resident for:

- five years or more*
- three to five years* → See Attachment A on Page 3
- less than three years → STOP → You are not eligible to apply for naturalization.

	True	Not True	
4. During the last five years, I have **not** been out of the United States for 30 months or more.	☐	☐ STOP →	For exceptions, see Attachment B on page 3.
5. During the last five years (or the last three years if I qualify under Attachment A), I have not taken a trip out of the United States that lasted one year or more.	☐	☐ STOP →	For exceptions, see Attachment C on page 3.
6. I have resided in the district or state in which I am applying for citizenship for the last three months.	☐	☐ STOP →	You must wait until you have lived in the state or district for three months to apply.
7. I can read, write and speak basic English.	☐	☐ STOP →	For exceptions, see Attachment D on page 4.
8. I know the fundamentals of U.S. history and the form and principles of the U.S. government.	☐	☐ STOP →	For exceptions, see Attachment E on page 4.

Go to Question 9.

*Naturalization applicants may file their applications 90 days before they have satisfied the "continuous residence" requirement.

Naturalization Eligibility Worksheet

	True	Not True	
9. I am a person of good moral character.	☐	☐ STOP →	You are not eligible to apply for naturalization.
10. One of the following is true: (a) I am female, **or** (b) I am a male registered with the Selective Service, **or** (c) I am a male who did not enter the United States under any status until after my 26th birthday, **or** (d) I am a male who was in the United States between the ages of 18 and 26 but who did not register with the Selective Service, and I will send a "Status Information Letter" from the Selective Service explaining why I did not register with my application. (e) I am a male who was in the United States between the ages of 18 and 26 as a lawful nonimmigrant.	☐	☐ STOP →	You are not eligible to apply for naturalization.
11. I have never deserted from the U.S. Armed Forces.	☐	☐ STOP →	You are not eligible to apply for naturalization.
12. I have never received an exemption or discharge from the U.S. Armed Forces on the grounds that I am an alien.	☐	☐ STOP →	You are not eligible to apply for naturalization.
13. I am willing to perform either military **or** civilian service for the United States if required by law. (**NOTE:** If your religious teachings and beliefs prohibit you from performing military service, you must be willing to perform non-military service.)	☐	☐ STOP →	You are not eligible to apply for naturalization.
14. I will support the Constitution of the United States.	☐	☐ STOP →	You are not eligible to apply for naturalization.
15. I understand and am willing to take an oath of allegiance to the United States.	☐	☐ STOP →	You are not eligible to apply for naturalization.

STOP HERE: You are probably eligible to apply for naturalization. Please call the Forms Line (1-800-870-3676) for an "Application for Naturalization" (Form N-400) and be sure to read *A Guide to Naturalization*.

Attachment A - Naturalization Eligibility Worksheet

I have been a Permanent Resident for three to five years

	True	Not True	
I am married to, and living with, a U.S. citizen.	☐	☐ STOP ►	You are not eligible to apply for naturalization.
I have been married to that U.S. citizen for at least the past three years.	☐	☐ STOP ►	You are not eligible to apply for naturalization.
My spouse has been a U.S. citizen for at least the past three years.	☐	☐ STOP ►	You are not eligible to apply for naturalization.
During the past three years, I have **not** been out of the country for 18 months or more.	☐	☐ STOP ►	You are not eligible to apply for naturalization.

If you answered "True" to all four questions, go to Question 5 on page 1.

Attachment B

I have been out of the country for 30 months or more

I am: (a) A person who has served on board a vessel operated by or registered in the United States, **or**

(b) An employee or an individual under contract to the U.S. Government, **or**

(c) A person who performs ministerial or priestly functions for a religious denomination or an interdenominational organization with a valid presence in the United States.

True ☐   Not True ☐ STOP ► You are not eligible to apply for naturalization.

If you answered "True," see pages 20 and 21 in *A Guide to Naturalization* to get more information and go to Question 5 on page 1.

Attachment C

I have been out of the country for one year or more

Since becoming a Permanent Resident, I have not taken a trip out of the United States that lasted for one year or more without an approved "Application to Preserve Residence for Naturalization Purposes" (Form N-470).

True ☐   Not True ☐ STOP ► You are not eligible to apply for naturalization.

NOTE: Only certain persons can use Form N-470. See Pages 18-21 in *A Guide to Naturalization* for more information.

If you answered "True," go to Question 6 on page 1.

Attachment D - Naturalization Eligibility Worksheet

I cannot read, write or speak basic English

	True	Not True	
I am over 50 years old and have lived in the United States for at least 20 years since I became a Permanent Resident, **or**	☐	☐ STOP →	You are not eligible to apply for naturalization.
I am over 55 years old and have lived in the United States for at least 15 years since I became a Permanent Resident, **or**	☐	☐ STOP →	You are not eligible to apply for naturalization.
I have a disability that prevents me from fulfilling this requirement and will be filing a "Medical Certification for Disability Exceptions" (Form N-648) completed and signed by a doctor with my application.	☐	☐ STOP →	You are not eligible to apply for naturalization.

NOTE: Only certain people can use this exemption. See pages 26 and 27 in *A Guide to Naturalization* for more information.

If you answered "True" to one of these questions, go to Question 8 on page 1.

Attachment E

I have a disability that prevents me from fulfilling the civics requirement

	True	Not True	
I have a disability that prevents me from fulfilling the civics requirement, and I will be filing "Medical Certification for Disability Exceptions" (Form N-648) completed and signed by a doctor with my application.	☐	☐ STOP →	You are not eligible to apply for naturalization.

NOTE: Only certain people can use this exemption. See pages 26 and 27 in *A Guide to Naturalization* for more information.

If you answered "True" to the question, go to Question 9 on page 2.

www.ingramcontent.com/pod-product-compliance
Lightning Source LLC
Chambersburg PA
CBHW081741170526
45167CB00009B/3896